The Story of Our Existence

María Sulbarán

BookLeaf Publishing

India | USA | UK

Presentation by *BookLeaf Publishing*

Web: www.bookleafpub.com

E-mail: info@bookleafpub.com

ISBN: 978-93-5744-972-4

First edition 2022

DEDICATION

For all those who feel too much.

ACKNOWLEDGEMENT

I want to start by thanking each and every one of
the people in my life who have given me a piece
of their existence to become the person I am
today. You made me.

Thanks to Bookleaf Publishing for allowing me
to realize one of the biggest dreams of my life.
This experience has changed me forever. Thank
you for putting part of my soul on these pages.

To the lady with heavenly eyes who put this
opportunity in front of me. Thank you for
teaching me that I am capable of doing much
more than I dare to do and for being the
inspiration for new words and feelings. I am
brighter with you.

To Bianca, who has been my partner in art for as
long as I can remember. Thank you for
absolutely everything you have done and
continue to do for me. I don't know where I
would be right now if it weren't for your
presence in my life. Thank you for creating
wonderful universes with me. Thank you for
believing in my abilities. Thank you for giving

me a chosen family. Thank you for teaching me that soulmates exist and can be found in a friend.

To my Mami Soledad, who has become my spiritual guide and best teacher. Thank you for always bringing me light in the dark and for showing me that love knows no time or distance.

To my mother, who is convinced that I could conquer the world if I set my mind to it. Thank you for supporting me, giving me the tools to be creative, and motivating me to explore my artistic side, even when you don't understand it most of the time.

To Mariangel, who is the best company to brainstorm. You were one of the first people with whom I dared to share my passion for writing, and this book would not exist without you. You are one of those friendships that happen once in your life. I believe in you as much as you have always believed in me.

To my sister, who always found a way to be present in my life despite the distance. Part of my soul is always with you. Thank you for being the most caring, supportive, unique, and talented big sister out there. I hope you are proud of me.

To Vitoria, who has been there for me since my life changed forever. Thank you for being an extraordinary friend, and for teaching me that existing is not enough to live. Most of the time you are my safe place and I will be forever grateful for that. Thank you for not leaving me alone.

To Leigh-Anne. I hope this book makes you feel less alone in the world. You are worthy of so much love and support. Never stop waking up everyday determined to reach your happy ending. You are stronger than anyone thinks. You are invincible. Thank you for supporting me every second of my life since we met.

To my father. Thank you for showing me how strong I actually am.

Thanks to Juliana, Fernanda, Sofia, Bryan, Paola, JP, Mãe Willma and the rest of my family for believing more in me than I ever did.

PREFACE

I feel a lot. I feel with depth and extraordinary passion. I am one of those people with a soul so heavy that sometimes it hurts to carry it inside. But at the same time, feeling the way I do has allowed me to connect with parts of myself that help me understand the strange beauty that life has.

Since I was little, I had problems expressing what I feel, since most of the time, I do not understand what I feel. My thoughts and words did not always live in harmony. It was not until I discovered the art of writing that I began to draw out everything accumulated within my being. Create worlds from my desires in which I can be and feel as I please. Writing allows me to explore parts of my mind that are typically unknown. It makes me feel seen, deciphered. And what I value most in the whole world; Writing helps me feel free.

As I feel a lot, I fear a lot, and I was always afraid to show this side of me to the world and realize that my words have no value. But when I was presented with the opportunity of writing this book, I decided to believe that words have the value that the writer gives them.

From the bottom of my heart, I hope to get to tell part of your story through mine.

The Purpose of My Eyes

I always wanted eyes
That could resemble
The sky.
Perhaps the ocean,
Or precious emeralds.
But my eyes, dark and young;
They are mirrors.
I learned to love
The uniqueness of their commonness.
They were created to reflect.
To resemble the
World around me.
For you to find
yourself in them.
To feel alive.
Seen.
Safe.
Someone
In the dark.

Oro, Mar Caribe y Sangre

Gold, sea and blood.
A rising firmament
Made up of young stars.
The most exquisite views
That could have been created.
But,
The gold is covered in blood.
My sister's blood runs through
My brother's hands.
My land seems wider,
Because it is emptying.
The stars are no longer
Reflected in my eyes.
Gold is no longer
Worth anything.
The sea no longer
Cleanses my body.
We have more blood
Than water to drink.
More bullets
Than bread to eat.
Chains, ocean and blood.

Chains, rage and blood.
Blood.

Hope.

From You, Not Yours

You built me
With all your broken parts
And extraordinary love.
You taught me to feel
Based on your existence.
You molded me to take the shape of your pride.
You gave me a vault as a home.
But not even the safest vault in the world
Could save me from the unthinkable of life.

I give you my heart as your home.
And I set you free from me.
I set myself free from you.
I set myself free from what does not belong to
me
From you.

Fire Behind the
Door

Do not close the door.
Do not blind me.
Do not hide the fire you have dragged me into.
Do not hide my ashes,
For they are also yours.
Do not steal the memories that should be mine.
Open the door.
Open it,
For I have forgotten how it feels to not be
burning alive
Behind closed doors,
Hoping that someone,
One day,
Will hear me cry.

I Choose to Belong

I belong to the land
That saw me grow.
I belong to the sky
That saw me leave.
I belong to the music
That made me exist.
I belong to your skin
That made me feel.
I belong to the memories
That I have owned.
I am from your lips
That nourish me,
From your eyes
That find me,
From the land
That takes care of me.
I belong to the dreams
I live for.
I belong to myself.
I am mine.
And I choose to live
In you.

Memory Garden

I remember the flowers in my garden.
I used to see them through my window.
Yellow roses.
Cayenne flower.
They were abundant and beautiful.
I remember them.
Roses,
White roses.
I used to see them
On the way home.
I had no windows.
I remember the flowers.
The flowers in my yard.
Roses.
Or perhaps daisies.
I remember a large tree
With leaves tinged with a yellow so vivid
And overwhelming
That it made my whole existence
Feel insignificant.
Flowers.
I can't remember flowers.
Perhaps there were never
Any flowers.

The Art That Conforms You

You are a sketch.
An imperfect work in constant transformation.
Every line, shape,
Curve and stain
That conforms you,
Seems flawed on their own.
But step away,
Watch the full picture.
You are in the process of becoming a
masterpiece.
Wonderfully unique.
The beauty of art
Can only be found through the eyes of the
viewer.
And only the artist knows the truth of their
work.
When you look in the mirror,
And you find the artist and the viewer,
You will be completed.

Make Me, Music

I can feel you so profoundly
As if you are part of me.
I find you in everything that surrounds me.
I find you in my emotions,
In every aspect of my being.
I see you transforming me,
Transforming the banalest and everyday things.
I hear you speak to me
In languages that I have never learned,
But somehow I understand you.
Somehow I know what you say.
We have the most momentous conversations
I have ever had the pleasure of being a part of.
Even though I never learned your language.
Even though I can not be through you,
I love to exist in this place.
In your world.
I am for you, and I feel you.
I hear you, music.
Make me.
I live in you.

Caged Bird

I am a caged bird.
My cage is spacious,
Comfortable,
Full of toys that should be enough
To make me happy.
My cage is full of laughter,
Love promises
And Anger.
It should be the perfect home.
My cage protects me.
I am safe.
But,
Birds are not meant to be in cages.
And sometimes I feel like I'm dying in here,
slowly and silently.
Alone.
Looking through the window.
Hoping…
I've already forgotten how to use my wings.

We Are Immensity

In a world in which your story
Was never part of mine,
I do not exist,
I do not know who I am.
This name belongs to someone,
With an entirely different life.
In a world in which your story,
Never changed mine,
Love did not become a concept
That I was able to define.
My passions remain unexplored,
And my creativity has nowhere to go.
I have no peace.
I have no home.
I am an orphan in soul.
In that world in which our existences
Never got to intersect,
Soulmate,
I am not.
I found you looking for myself,
and now I keep finding pieces
Of myself in you.
In this world
You are in me.
I am in you.

And although we can be without the other,
We are immensity.
Soulmate,
We found us.

Nobody's Door

The door is open,
But nobody sees me leave.
Nobody asks how long I have been gone.
Nobody misses me.
The burns that mark my entire body
Are wholly ignored.
I walk through a crowd of people
Feeling like a ghost,
Dragging chains on my feet
That no one offers to help me carry.
And then I think that maybe
Only I feel them.
Maybe only I see them.
No one else can imagine the pain of my burns,
For only my body knows them.
Nobody sees me.
Nobody sees the door.
Nobody knows it exists.
Nobody knows I am alone.

Incompatible Maps

We both became experts at hurting each other.
You are my greatest weakness.
And I am your reflection.
We are both lost right now,
Reading maps with different directions.
I want more than anything to find you,
To decipher you.
Hold you close to me,
And decide when to let you go.
I love you with such immense depth
That it hurts in every part of me.
I miss you.
I dream of you every night,
And I know,
Deep inside me,
That I am close to having you
In a way I never did before.

I Set Me Free

I set you free.
Run,
You can leave now.
I solemnly swear to take care of you
Until my last breath of life.
I say goodbye forever,
And I take the pain from you.
I promise to remember you.
To always keep you close to me.
The door is open.
My sweet little girl,
I set you free.

Your Existence in Mine

The night I found you
Your name echoed tirelessly in my head.
When I pronounced you,
My mouth was filled with an extraordinary
sensation.
You tasted sweet.
Familiar on my lips.
I've known your name all my life.

When I saw your eyes,
Beautiful and immense,
I found answers to questions that only my soul
knew.
I found what I had given up looking for.
You found me in pieces,
With a heart full of love with no place to go.
And when you held my hand,
My entire body was on fire.
But darling,
Fire never felt so exquisite against my skin.

Nice to Meet You Again

I knew you more than you knew yourself.
You knew me more than I wanted you to.
Eventually,
We memorized each other entirely.
I knew you just as you knew yourself.
You knew me just as I wanted you to.
But when I woke up that morning,
And I noticed that I had lost all trace of you in
my memory,
I felt like I was going to disappear.
My whole world lost its meaning
Because knowing you was the only thing
I had ever been sure of in my life.
I was so afraid of losing you,
That I forgot what the purpose of having you
was.
Oh, soulmate,
When I went to sleep one night
And felt peace in not knowing you,
I cried until I was dry.
I cried consumed with so much joy,
discovering that meeting you again

Was the most ethereal wonder.
Now you know who you are.
Now I know who I am.

The Beginning of Us

You once told me
That I provoked a frozen fire inside of you.
And I feel it.
I feel the heat that consumes me.
I feel the cold that paralyzes me.
It makes me tremble
I feel everything inside of me blooming.
Nourishing me.
Giving me new life.
I feel so much.
Feelings that barely learn to exist in me.
And I feel things that can not be described,
Because they only exist in this absurd,
And absolutely beautiful world
That you have created
Inside of me.

You Left Your Name on Me

My skin now bears your name.
With your lips, you have undone me,
And you have created something new.
Something ours.
I am at your mercy.
Your lips,
A blessed curse,
Have saved me.
All trace of darkness in my being has
disappeared.
Instead,
There is a fire inside me
That warms me, never burning.
I'm light.
I'm endless.
I am alive.
So divinely alive.
Your fingers play this new melody
That is my desire.
Your body is music to me.
I never knew I longed to hear it.
Darling, I want to learn it.

I want to know it by heart
And replay it in my head until I am stunned.
With your eyes, I feel condemned.
You make me a prisoner.
Your words are torture.
And what a sweet condemnation.
Oh, such pleasurable torture.
My present now bears your name,
For I never felt so close
To it like I do now.

To Feel and Be Felt

I feel the weight of the entire universe
Inside my chest.
I feel the brightness of the stars,
The colors of the sky,
The fluttering of butterflies.
I feel with the immensity
Of anything capable of destroying
Everything in its path.
I feel your words in the depths of my being.
I feel your eyes on me.
Perceiving me.
I always wanted to stop feeling.
But,
As my existence expands,
I have come to realize that feeling is what makes
me be.
I was born to feel,
and hopefully,
To be felt.

Surviving the Future

I am at the bottom of the ocean.
Drowning.
Still learning how to swim.
I get close to the surface,
Just enough to fill my lungs with oxygen
Before being consumed by the next wave.
I don't see clearly where I'm going,
But I feel it.
I am exhausted.
I am thirsty.
But I refuse to die here.
I don't know where I am,
But I know where I should be.
And I keep going.
I'm still learning.
I don't know the strength of the next wave to
come,
But I know I can bear it.
I will arrive.
I know this will be worth diving here.
I'm going to live.

Heaven

I've never been one for religion.
Skipped church on Christmas.
Don't think I missed much,
But now I'm committed.

She makes me feel holy.
The pearly gates, laid open.
I scream, I'm devoted.
Please, let me inside.

At her feet I worship.
Good lord, this is worth it.
She gives me a taste
Of the angelic divine.

I can hardly believe it.
I'm on my knees, pleading.
She leaves her mark now,
To tell me "you're mine."

Suddenly sinless.
I'm washed clean, beg permission.
My lady grants me mercy,
Becoming further entwined.

She makes prayers come easy.
Love me, love sweetly.
Don't stop now.
Forever complete me.

- Honey B.

Yesterday's Dreams

Once I had a dream
Where I leaned in
And whispered in your ear to say:
"I need you to warm up every part of me."
You said:
"If I could, I would be purring."
I get goosebumps every time you
Shift against my side.
I go still and shiver again.
I am undone,
Surely with a look of shock still plastered on my
face.
Lightly tracing fingers very slowly
Begin to go lower.
End your path on the inside of my left thigh.
The firm touch feels like a statement.
I'm too warm to have goosebumps now,
But I still shiver.
Your thumb again
Awakening parts of me.
It's a love letter,
But I'm not sure where it ends.

- Honey B.

www.ingramcontent.com/pod-product-compliance
Lightning Source LLC
Chambersburg PA
CBHW070615160726
48003CB00005B/2297